The Wild West in American History

GUNFIGHTERS

Written by Leonard J. Matthews
Illustrated by Roger Payne and others
Edited by Arlene Rourke

Library of Congress Cataloging-in-Publication Data

Matthews, Leonard.
  Gunfighters.

  (The Wild West in American history)
  Summary: Traces the lives of some of the Old West's most colorful
lawmen and desperados, including Wild Bill Hickok, Billy the Kid, and
John Wesley Hardin.
  1. Outlaws—United States—History—19th century—Juvenile
literature. 2. Frontier and pioneer life—West (U.S.)—Juvenile
literature. 3. West (U.S.)—History—1848-1950—Juvenile literature.
[1. Robbers and outlaws. 2. Peace officers—West (U.S.) 3. Frontier and
pioneer life. 4. West (U.S.)—History]
I. Rourke, Arlene, 1944-   . II. Title. III. Series.
F596.M335   1988   976'.041'0922   [920]   87-20479
ISBN 0-86625-361-0

Rourke Publications, Inc.
Vero Beach, Florida, 32964

The Wild West in American History
GUNFIGHTERS

GUNFIGHTERS

Movies and Western books have gone a long way toward creating myths about the Old West. Most people think that the era of the gunfighters went on for a very long time. In fact, the day of the "shootists" (as they were called in their own time) was very brief. It can be said that the period ran from 1865, the end of the Civil War and the start of the great trail herds, to the late 1880s.

Before the end of the century, progress had overtaken the gunfighter. Outlaws, such as Butch Cassidy and the Sundance Kid, found that their riding days were gone forever. The wide open ranges belonged to the past. Barbed wire fences put an end to bandits on fast horses outgalloping their pursuers across rolling prairies.

Even science conspired against them. The telephone was now in everyday use. That meant that news of a robbery could be transmitted instantly to law officers in the area. Robbers attempting a quick escape were more easily followed and captured.

For a brief period, the gunfighter was king of the Old West. This book relates the deeds of some of the more colorful members.

WILD BILL HICKOK

$\mathcal{J}$ames Butler Hickok, to call him by his real name, was born on May 27, 1837, in Homer, Illinois. Homer was later renamed Troy Creek. Hickok was only eighteen when he first ran into trouble. He quarrelled with a teamster and, during the fistfight that followed, they both fell into a canal. Hickok scrambled out safely, but there was no sign of the teamster. Hickok mistakenly believed that the man had drowned and lost no time in leaving the district.

The next time Jim Hickok surfaced, he was in Kansas. It was 1855 and Kansas was a hotbed of treachery and wholesale killing. The seeds of the Civil War were being sown among the pro- and anti-slavery factions. Hickok favored the anti-slavery forces and joined the Free State Army.

In 1861, the Civil War broke out and Hickok left Kansas for Nebraska. He took a job in Rock Creek as a stock tender with the Pony Express and the Overland Express Station. It was at the station that Hickok got into serious trouble with the law.

A farmer named David McCanles and the station manager, Horace Wellman, had argued fiercely about a debt owed to McCanles by the company which owned the Pony Express. McCanles was accompanied by two friends. It was claimed that all three men were unarmed.

Suddenly, the argument erupted into violence. A shot was fired and McCanles fell dead. More shots rang out and his two friends lay dead. Reports differ as to whether it was Hickok or Wellman who fired the shots. Apparently, there was enough suspicion to go around because the sheriff arrested both Hickok and Wellman, together with Wellman's wife and a stable hand named Brink. All four were charged with murder and hauled before the judge. Astonishingly, all four were released on the grounds of self-defense.

With a carving knife and two .36 caliber Navy revolvers, Wild Bill was ready for any sudden attack.

Hickok lost no time hitting the trail out of Rock Creek. Three months afterward, he joined the Union Army as a wagon master.

The Civil War was now raging full force and, once again, it intruded into Hickok's life. He fought in the battle of Wilson's Creek in Missouri. He went on to serve as a scout and spy. It was during this time that he acquired the famous nickname "Wild Bill." Perhaps he earned it because of his daring exploits during the war. Or perhaps Jim was called Wild Bill in contrast to his older brother, Lorenzo, who was known as "Tame Bill."

At the end of the war, Wild Bill was in Springfield, Missouri. He was gambling with a friend named Dave Tutt. There was an argument over a gambling debt. Tutt snatched Hickok's watch from the gambling table, saying that he would keep it in payment for the money Hickok owed him. Hickok warned Tutt never to use the watch if he valued his life.

Dave Tutt should have known that Hickok would make good his threat. The next day, Tutt displayed the watch in the public square. Wild Bill Hickok was not a man to be mocked. Guns blazed. Tutt missed. Hickok did not.

Wild Bill was charged with murder for the second time. Later, the charge was reduced to manslaughter. Luck was still with him. He was acquitted and released.

Hickok returned briefly to military life. It was during this time he was befriended by the famous Civil War general and frontier fighter, George Armstrong Custer. Custer had heard of Wild Bill's exploits and admired him.

The year 1869 found Hickok, never able to settle down for long, in Hays City, Kansas. At the time, Hays City was crowded with railroad laborers, cowboys, and soldiers from the garrison. Perhaps the law-abiding citizens of Hays City felt the need of a strong, experienced gunman to act as sheriff.

They certainly got experience when they elected Wild Bill sheriff. Soon enough, he was in the thick of the action. On August 24, a man named Bill Melvin and two of his ruffian friends started shooting up the town. Sheriff Hickok shot Melvin dead.

A month later, Hickok was called into a saloon to settle a disturbance. It ended in the death of another man, Sam Strawhun. Saloon patrons grew to be very wary whenever Sheriff Hickok entered.

In July of 1870, Hickok was beaten up in a saloon by some troopers of the 7th Cavalry once commanded by General Custer. Hard hit though he was, Hickok managed to draw his pistol. One trooper dropped in his tracks, dead. Another trooper staggered away, badly wounded.

By now, Wild Bill was ready to pull out of Hays City. He set out for Abilene, Kansas. On April 15, 1871, he was appointed city marshal. Abilene was not any kinder to Bill than Hays City had been.

Phil Coe owned a saloon in town. He was also a gambler and able gunman. A feud developed between the two men. It festered for a while until it finally exploded in gunfire. Hickok mortally wounded Coe. Hearing footsteps behind him, Hickok thought it was one of Coe's friends trying to take him from the back. In a split second, he turned and fired. Horrified, he realized too late that the man he had shot was his good friend and deputy, Mike Williams.

Tired of a life of gunslinging, Wild Bill joined Buffalo Bill Cody's theatrical troupe. Show business wasn't for him, and he soon quit.

One day, he was sitting at a gambling table in Deadwood, South Dakota. He was busy playing cards and didn't notice the young drifter behind him. Jack McCall pulled out his gun and shot Hickok in the back. He was hanged for the cold-blooded murder. He never revealed why he committed the crime. Perhaps he wanted to be the man who shot Wild Bill Hickok.

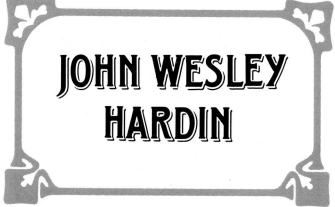

JOHN WESLEY HARDIN

John Wesley Hardin was a handsome young man with a steely, relentless gaze. Any gunmen foolish enough to challenge him had only to stare into Hardin's ice-cold eyes glaring across a loaded revolver to know that the sands of time were running out quickly for them.

Strangely enough, this young desperado was named after a man of God. The original John Wesley was the founder of the Methodist religion. That is why, when a son was born to the Reverend and Mrs. J.G. Hardin, they named the boy John Wesley Hardin.

If his parents had hoped that little John would grow up to teach wicked men the error of their ways, as his namesake had done, they were sadly mistaken. The only lesson that many suicidal men facing him learned was that he could draw faster than they could.

Wes Hardin was born on May 26, 1853, in Bonham, Texas. The next twelve years were troubled ones for Texas. Political unrest over the issue of slavery was brewing between the states. The Northern states wanted to free the slaves and the Southern states wanted to retain slavery. A bitter war followed. In 1865 the North won, but savage dislike between the North and South continued.

One day, in the street, twelve-year-old Wes quarrelled with a black boy named Mage. Wes ordered Mage to step aside so that Wes could pass. Mage refused. Harsh words followed and Mage struck at young Hardin with a club. Instantly, Hardin drew a revolver and shot Mage dead.

Wes Hardin fled, pursued by three cavalrymen bent on capturing him. Thinking that he might not be able to outrun them, he waited for them in ambush. Three shots rang out. Three troopers lay dead.

In post-Civil War Texas, shooting a black boy and three Northern soldiers was not considered a crime. Unbelievable as it may seem, Wes Hardin was teaching class in a school in Pisga only a few months later. Pisga was in Novarro County, Texas. His father had recently been appointed head of the school.

By his own account, young Wes was a satisfactory tutor. Wes had two cousins, Tom Dixon, and Manning Clements who later became a well-known rancher. The boys were setting out on the trail one day to round up longhorns. After three months of teaching, Wes decided to join them.

Soon afterward, Wes was accused of another crime. This time, there was no doubt as to his innocence. Even so, he fled, pursued again by Northern troopers. He was overtaken and once more bloodshed followed. Two cavalrymen died under his guns.

John Wesley Hardin was now a very much wanted outlaw. He was only sixteen, but he was reputed to be one of the most dangerous killers in Texas. Now a hunted criminal, he lived a life of constant violence. Murder came easily to him.

In May 1872, he married Jane Bowen, the pretty daughter of a rancher. But his years as an

John Wesley Hardin, the terror of Texas. He feared no man.

outlaw were coming to an end.

With thirty or more killings behind him, John Wesley Hardin shot a man in a saloon. Again he ran, this time to Florida.

He was arrested, tried, and sentenced to twenty-five years in prison. He actually served only fifteen years of his sentence before being released with a full pardon. His wife was now dead, leaving a son and two daughters. Perhaps it was because of them that Hardin decided to stop his life of violence and finally settle down.

It was not to be. His past was too much with him.

It was August, 1895. Hardin was gambling in a saloon in El Paso, Texas. John Sellman, the chief peace officer, entered the saloon. Without a word of explanation, he took out his gun and shot Hardin in the back, killing him.

COMMODORE PERRY OWENS

Commodore Perry Owens and John Wesley Hardin were similar in three respects. Both were handsome. Both were named after famous men, and both were fast on the draw. In one respect they were not alike. Commodore Perry Owens was a lawman who believed that the law should be respected and obeyed. John Wesley Hardin thought the law was a nuisance and ignored it.

Little is known of Commodore Perry Owens's parents and childhood. His parents must certainly have admired the original Commodore Matthew Galbraith Perry who commanded the U.S. Navy during the latter half of the Mexican War.

Owens was a tall man with yellow hair, as handsome as a Greek god. He never drank, gambled or smoked, and he had a faultless respect for women. He wore his hair very long.

Commodore Perry Owens's first recorded appearance was as a horse guard at the stage station in Navajo Springs, Arizona. He soon won the grudging respect of the Indians who did their best to run off the horses he was guarding. Once they tried to ambush him. It resulted in four dead Indians. Another story goes that Owens was besieged in the station by more than one hundred Indians. He stood them off for three days until they gave up.

After several years of pointless skirmishes, the Indians finally left him alone.

Life in Arizona in the 1880s was far from peaceful. Troubles erupted between the Americans, the Mexicans, and the Indians. Feuds between families led to all-out warfare.

Pleasant Valley held two such warring families, the Grahams and the Tewksburys. The war began when the Tewksburys drove their sheep into the valley, for cattlemen and sheepherders were bitter enemies.

During this time of turmoil, Navajo County was formed and Holbrook was named as the county capital. Everyone agreed that they needed a sheriff. The position was offered to and accepted by Commodore Perry Owens.

A third family, named Blevins, joined the Pleasant Valley war. Old man Blevins deliberately made an enemy of Owens. It ended in a shootout. The old man and two of his five sons were killed by Owens. The remaining sons joined the Graham family.

War and bloodshed continued until the brutality of the Blevins brothers turned the Grahams against them. In disgust, the Blevins and a notorious rustler named Mose Roberts pulled out and headed for greener pastures. Before leaving, the Blevins brothers decided to visit their mother. Sheriff Owens had warned

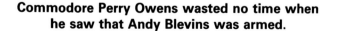

Commodore Perry Owens wasted no time when he saw that Andy Blevins was armed.

them to stay away from Holbrook. When news came to him that they were back and uttering threats against him, he quietly loaded his guns and set out.

The Blevins home was crowded that day. With Mrs. Blevins were her three sons, Andy (alias Cooper), the oldest, and the two younger boys, Johnny and Sam. The rustler Roberts (who was also their brother-in-law), the wife of Johnny Blevins, and a Mrs. Gladden and her nine-year-old daughter were also there.

Owens stopped outside the house and called on Andy and his brothers to surrender. Andy appeared, gun in hand. Inside, Johnny, Sam, and Roberts prepared for battle. The fight lasted only a minute, but when Owens rode away unhurt, he left behind him Andy, Sam, and Roberts dead and Johnny badly wounded. The whole of Arizona learned that there was no trifling with Commodore Perry Owens.

He died peacefully in 1919, an honored and highly respected man.

CLAY ALLISON

If ever there was a wild one, it was Robert A. Clay Allison. Allison was born in Waynesboro, Wayne County, Tennessee, in 1840. Some people speculate that the irrational behavior he displayed all his life was due to a blow to the head which he received in his childhood.

He was only twenty-one when the Civil War broke out. He enlisted in the Tennessee Light Artillery, fighting for the Southern cause. After only three months of service, he was discharged for his strange behavior. The Confederate army might have figured that it was finished with Clay Allison, but he had not finished with the army. Undaunted, he re-enlisted. This time he chose the cavalry. He fought with them until the end of the war.

After getting out of the army, Allison went to Texas looking for work. He was hired as a trailherder by two famous cattlemen, Oliver

Wyatt Earp and his deputy Bat Masterson were the lawmen of Dodge City.

Loving and Charles Goodnight. Tales of his misdeeds and irresponsible ways began to circulate. As is so often the case with wild men in wild times, rumors flew thick and fast.

A near-explosion occurred in Dodge City, Kansas, when Allison came across Wyatt Earp and Bat Masterson. Earp and Masterson were lawmen in Dodge at the time.

Sure it is that Allison never did like town marshals. He liked them even less if they were Yankees, which both Earp and Masterson were. The very sight of those two stalking the street would have been enough cause for Clay to keep his guns loaded.

Clay Allison, a ruthless gunman with a hair-trigger temper.

That the three men met seems certain. The fact that Allison rode out of town and none of them was wounded would indicate that no gunplay took place. Perhaps Earp and Masterson were not unfriendly toward Clay and sought no quarrel. This may have been one of the few times that Clay was able to keep his temper in check. Lucky it was too, for when he was aroused he could — and did — kill ruthlessly.

His ever uncertain temper reached fever point when a weeping woman came to Clay and told him that her husband, a rancher named Charles Kennedy, had just killed their infant daughter. The distraught mother went on to tell Allison that her husband was in the habit of murdering any lonely traveler who happened to stop off at the ranch asking for a night's lodging.

This brutal behavior on Kennedy's part infuriated Allison. He gathered some other desperate characters and raced toward the ranch.

Clay Allison was fond of shooting up peaceful towns and scaring the townsfolks.

They awakened the sleeping rancher and hauled him off to jail. Later some bones were dug up outside the Kennedy cabin. Allison and his gang decided not to wait for a court trial. They stormed the jail, took Kennedy outside, and hanged him.

Normally, Clay Allison did not go out looking for trouble. Left alone, he was a quiet enough man. Every once in a while though, he would start feeling bored. To relieve his pent-up emotions, he would ride through town, guns blazing. It was very dangerous to be on the street when Allison was in town. Even the lawmen didn't try to stop him. It would be like trying to stop a herd of stampeding cattle.

Unlucky was the man against whom he nursed a grievance. There was the time when he rode into Cheyenne with a herd of cattle. He was nursing a painful toothache, and sought out a dentist. By mistake, the dentist pulled the wrong tooth. Furious, Allison found another dentist who removed the right tooth. The crisis over, Allison returned to the first dentist. Hurling the man into a chair, Allison tore a tooth out of the man's jaw and was only prevented from ripping out all his teeth by the arrival of an outraged band of citizens.

Sooner or later, a man with a reputation such as Allison's was bound to meet up with another of the same breed. When that happened it followed that they had to prove who was the better man.

One afternoon Clay Allison was eating in a restaurant seated opposite an ugly customer named Chunk Colbert. Chunk already had seven killings behind him. He did not live long enough to make it eight. Foolishly he slipped his gun out of its holster when he thought Clay was not watching and aimed it under the table. When he fired, the bullet was deflected and missed Allison who did not make the same error. Colbert died and Clay went on quietly with his meal.

In the end, he died at the age of 47 as a result of an accident. He tripped one day, and fell from a wagon he was loading. The nervous horses moved forward, and the wagon ran over Clay, breaking his neck and back.

JESSE JAMES

If there was anything Jesse James liked better than robbing banks, it was holding up trains.

esse James was one of two brothers born to Robert and Zerelda James in Clay County, Missouri. His older brother, Alexander Frank, was born in 1843. Jesse was born in 1847. Both brothers earned well deserved reputations as merciless bandits. Jesse was the worse of the two.

At the outbreak of the Civil War in 1861, Frank left home and struck out on his own. By the age of twenty, he was riding with a band of guerillas led by one of the most blood-thirsty men ever to straddle a saddle. His name was William Clarke Quantrell.

During this time, Jesse stayed home with his mother. His father had died when he was five years old and his mother had married a man named Dr. Reuben Samuel.

One day, several armed men rode up to the Samuel homestead. They said they were looking for Frank. They claimed to be from the Kansas Militia, owing allegiance to the North. When Dr. Samuel told them he did not know Frank's whereabouts, they tortured him. They whipped Jesse and his mother. Having learned nothing, they rode away.

A bitter hatred rose in Jesse's heart as he watched them leave. He vowed to have revenge. Revenge took the form of joining his brother and Quantrell's guerillas.

It was while Frank and Jesse were members of Quantrell's ruthless gang that they met two other brothers who were to share their future notoriety, Cole and Jim Younger.

To his partners in crime, Jesse was known as "Dingus." The story goes that one day, while practicing his marksmanship, he accidently shot off the top of one of his fingers. "By Dingus! I shot myself!" he yelled. From then on, he was Dingus to all of them.

It was 1865, the last year of the war. Jesse had been shot and badly wounded in one of the gang's raids. He was nursed by his cousin, who bore the same first name as his mother, Zerelda Mimms. Jesse never forgot Zerelda's care and attention. Ten years later they were married.

Those were bad days for the people of Missouri. They had sided with the South in the war and the South had lost. In punishment, they were attacked and driven from their homes. There was much bitterness toward Northerners and much admiration for anyone who would fight back against the Northerners. That is why the James and Younger brothers, outlaws though they were, could find help and shelter from the law.

Jesse James was known to all his friends as Dingus.

By this time, Jesse and Frank had been fighting and raiding for too long ever to settle down to peaceful lives. They were used to being outlaws. Two other Younger brothers, Bob and John joined the gang.

In May of 1865, a month after the war ended, Quantrell was ambushed by Union soldiers and killed. Nine months later, Jesse led a band of raiders into the town of Liberty, Missouri. Guns blazing, they smashed their way into the First National Bank and made off with $15,000 in gold coins. As they rode away, they killed a young college student who was standing in the street.

This was the first bank robbery to take place in the United States. It created a sensation. Triumphantly, Jesse planned fresh raids. Lexington, Missouri, and Richmond, Missouri, were pinpointed as future targets. Soon their safes were emptied under the threatening guns of the James/Younger gang.

For several years, the gang continued to rob banks throughout Missouri. Then, on July 23, 1873, they changed their tactics.

They robbed a train in Iowa. Disappointed, they rode off with only $7,000. Later they found out that they had robbed the wrong train. Quick to correct their error, they headed for the Gads Hill depot in Missouri to wait for the arrival of the Iron Mountain Express. To be sure that there was no interference, they herded all the honest citizens into the depot building. With no one to stop them, they held up the train and made a clean getaway.

They might not have realized it, but time was running out for the James/Younger gang. The famous Pinkerton Detective Agency was put on their trail. Soon afterward, John Younger was killed by a Pinkerton man.

It was in Northfield, Minnesota, that the James and Younger brothers rode together for the last time. On one of their raids, the local residents fought back. Two outlaws, Clell Miller and Bill Chadwell, were shot dead. Jim, Bob, and Cole Younger were wounded and rounded up two weeks later.

Frank and Jesse managed to escape. Both went into hiding. Jesse went to live with his wife and two children.

Still eager for action, Jesse planned a new robbery. He enlisted the aid of his two cousins, Bob and Charlie Ford. Now there was a price on his head: $25,000 reward for the death or capture of Jesse James. All that money was just too tempting for Bob Ford. Jesse James, probably the best known of all the Western outlaws, was shot in the back of the head while hanging a picture on his bedroom wall.

In 1882, the same year Jesse died, Frank James surrendered to the law. He served time in prison and died a free man in February, 1915.

Jesse should have known better than to take off his guns and turn his back on an armed man.

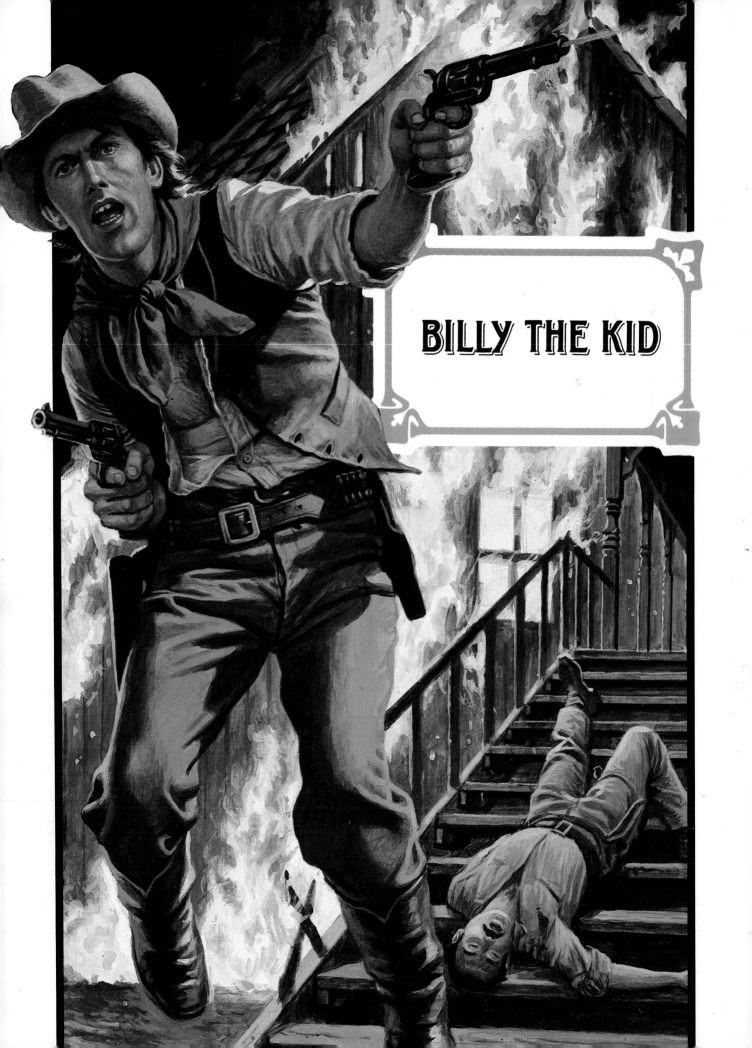

BILLY THE KID

$\mathcal{B}$illy the Kid's days as a gunfighter began in the little township of Lincoln County, New Mexico, in 1877. He drifted into town alone, looking for a job. For some unknown reason, an English rancher and storeowner named John Tunstall took a liking to him and hired him as a ranch hand.

Billy's past was murky, to say the least. There are few reliable facts. It was said that his father died when Billy was very young. He and his widowed mother drifted from town to town and state to state until finally settling in Silver City, New Mexico.

In Santa Fe on March 1, 1873, Billy's mother married a former private in the Indiana Volunteer Infantry. His name was William H. Antrim. Billy's real name was Henry, so for some time he was known as Henry Antrim.

Billy was about fifteen when his mother died. Soon after that, he started to get into trouble. He was accused of helping a no-good character named Sombrero Jack to steal some clothes from two Chinese people. He was arrested and thrown in jail. Somehow he managed to escape and fled to Arizona.

Known as Kid Antrim, he worked on a ranch. It was at this time that Billy killed his first man. The man, E.P. Cahill, was a bully who thought that the undersized whelp would be easily cowed. He was wrong. A bitter quarrel ensued. Then came a fistfight. Billy was knocked to the ground. He saw Cahill coming at him again. Quickly, he whipped out his gun and shot Cahill dead.

Billy was arrested again, this time for murder. True to form, again he escaped from jail. He bolted to Lincoln, New Mexico, and it was there that he was called Billy the Kid and met John Tunstall. Tunstall was in a tough situation. Rashly, he had opened a store in Lincoln. He took as his partner a lawyer named Alexander McSween. A competitive store in town was run by three crafty, ruthless men named Laurence G. Murphy, James J. Dolan, and John H. Riley. They were involved in cattle rustling and shady political activities. They were not standing for competition from an Englishman and a slick lawyer.

On the trumped-up charge of an unpaid debt, they laid claim to some of Tunstall's horses. They sent men to round up the horses.

This young man was known by many names but it was as Billy the Kid that he was known throughout the United States.

John Tunstall tried to stop them. He was shot dead in cold blood. Watching all this was an undersized, buck-toothed rider called Billy.

Billy escaped and swore revenge. A posse was formed to capture the killers. Two were taken into custody. Billy shot both of them.

One killing followed another as the feud continued. One night Billy and several other Tunstall/McSween followers were trapped in McSween's house by their enemies. The house was set on fire. Billy begged McSween and his wife to make a break for it. Billy loaded his guns. McSween led the way and was shot dead. Behind him, Billy herded the others out of the burning building. Harvey Morris, a law student working in McSween's office, was then killed, but all the others escaped.

By now, there had been so many men killed on both sides in Lincoln, the dispute had become known as the Lincoln County War. At this time, a new governor· of New Mexico was elected. He was a former major general in the Civil War. His name was Lew Wallace, the author of the novel *Ben Hur*.

Wallace tried to bring peace to Lincoln County. One of his first acts was to send word to Billy the Kid that the governor would guarantee his safety, if he surrendered.

Billy accepted the governor's promise. He turned himself in and handed over his guns. Unfortunately, the District Attorney, William R. Rynerson, was a friend of Billy's enemies. He ignored the governor's pardon and tried to prosecute Billy anyway.

Once again, Billy broke out of jail. This is one of the few times in Billy's life that the records as to his whereabouts are precise. On January 10, 1880, Billy showed up in a saloon in Fort Sumner, New Mexico. Wherever the Kid went, there was trouble. A brawl led to a gunfight, and another man lay dead at Billy's feet.

Later that year, a peace officer named Pat Garrett drifted into Lincoln. He was a tall and deliberate man. His mission was to catch Billy. Twice Garrett cornered the Kid, leaving bloodshed behind. Finally, in December 1880, Garrett captured the Kid.

Billy was taken to Mesilla, New Mexico. There he stood trial for the murder of Sheriff Brady, who had been ambushed and shot not long after the Tunstall killing. Although there was no actual proof that Billy had committed the murder, he was sentenced to death and taken to Lincoln to be hanged.

The rope was never braided that would hang Billy the Kid. One day, he killed his two guards and made his last escape.

Three months later, word reached Pat Garrett that Billy was hiding in Fort Sumner. Garrett went there and hid in the house of Pete Maxwell, an informer against Billy. At midnight, Billy crept into the house. In the darkness, he did not see Garrett, but Garrett saw him. He was not about to give Billy the Kid another chance to escape. He shot the Kid right through the heart.

WYATT EARP

The names of Earp and Tombstone will be linked forever. It was in the town of Tombstone in October 1881 that three Earp brothers with their friend, Doc Holliday, headed toward the O.K. Corral for a showdown with their sworn enemies, the Clanton brothers and the McLaury brothers.

As is so often the case, the golden-haired superman of legend is quite different from the real man. So it is with Wyatt Earp.

His full name was Wyatt Berry Stapp Earp. He was born in 1848 in Monmouth, Illinois. First he tried his hand on the right side of the law. In 1870 he was elected a peace officer in Lamar County, Missouri. He did not find life as a lawman interesting enough to detain him for long.

In 1871 he was arrested for horse stealing in Oklahoma. He paid a bail of $500 and fled the territory before being brought to trial. In 1874 he was in Wichita, again serving as a lawman. This spell of honesty did not last long, however. Soon he was in trouble for refusing to turn over fines he had collected from lawbreakers. Again Earp was forced to hit the road.

The years 1876 to 1879 found him in Dodge City, Kansas. There he balanced two conflicting professions, assistant marshal and professional gambler. You might say that he had it both ways — nobody was ever going to accuse the deputy marshal of cheating at cards.

Alongside Wyatt Earp in Dodge City was his Indian-fighter friend, Bat Masterson. Despite Earp's lawless tendencies, he managed to keep everyone else in line. In fact, Earp and Masterson earned a reputation for being tough on lawbreakers. Earp was quick on the draw and took no nonsense from anyone.

In December 1879, Wyatt and his two

Any man who drew a gun in a Dodge City saloon was very close to certain death if Wyatt Earp happened to be present.

brothers, Morgan and Virgil, arrived in Tombstone, Cochise County, Arizona. The town had been named by Ed Schieffelin, a prospector who had discovered a rich silver lode there. After a lucky strike, he named his diggings Tombstone. It was a rough town and Earp had been warned that all he was likely to find there was a tombstone.

Cochise County was one of the most lawless areas in the West. Roughnecks and killers robbed stages, rustled cattle, and terrorized law-abiding citizens.

Virgil Earp was appointed town marshal of Tombstone. From time to time, his brothers Wyatt and Morgan acted as his deputies. Two years after the Earps hit town, the governor of Arizona reported to the Secretary of State that much of the blame for the continued lawlessness in Tombstone could be leveled at the local peace officers.

The governor visited Tombstone and talked with the county sheriff, John Behan. Behan complained that Virgil Earp was not co-operating with him in bringing the wrongdoers to justice. Virgil made the same complaint against Behan.

Trouble was boiling and the Earps readied themselves for gunplay. A friend of theirs had recently joined them in Tombstone. His name

Wyatt Earp whose name will always be linked with the gunfight at the O.K. corral.

was John Holliday. He was a gambling dentist, who spent more time drawing aces than pulling teeth. He was well known throughout the West by his nickname, "Doc." Doc was a skillful gunman and a valuable ally in any gunfight.

On October 26, 1881, an armed group of rustlers, the Clantons and the McLaurys, arrived in Tombstone. They had known the Earps in another town and had quarrelled bitterly with them.

The Earps and Doc Holliday set out to arrest these rustlers. Sheriff Behan attempted to stop them, but they brushed him aside. A short, but deadly, gunfight took place. It has gone down in history as the "Gunfight at the O.K. Corral." In fact, it took place on the street some distance from the corral. In less than a minute both McLaurys and Billy Clanton were dead. Doc Holliday, Virgil, and Morgan Earp were wounded. Only Ike Clanton and Wyatt Earp survived the fight without a scratch.

Despite his lawless ways, Wyatt Earp died peacefully in bed in 1929.

*B*utch Cassidy knew that some day he might like to take a trip abroad. Cassidy was not a man to save up for such things, as a normal person would. No, he was always attracted to the lawless approach.

With the aid of several other outlaws, he held up a train. It was a successful raid — or so it seemed at the time. There was just one difficulty; although the take amounted to some $65,000 in currency, all the bills were new and not one of them had been signed officially by the bank!

They were worthless. If Butch Cassidy had been a better student, this incident might have taught him something about the pointlessness of leading a life of crime. Unfortunately, Butch had to learn his lessons the hard way.

Cassidy was one of the leading members in a gang of outlaws called "The Wild Bunch," a name given to them by the newspapers in the

THE WILD BUNCH

The Wild Bunch were wanted for holding up trains but they were not always as successful as they wished.

area they were rustling. They were also known as "The Long Riders" and "The Hole in the Wall Gang." This last name came from the Hole in the Wall Valley, which was one of the places at which they gathered before a robbery.

Nicknames were commonplace among the Wild Bunch. "Butch Cassidy's" real name was Robert Leroy Parker. Harry Longbaugh was known as the "Sundance Kid." Ben Kilpatrick was referred to as the "Tall Texan." George Curry was "Flatnose," for an obvious reason. Hard-of-hearing Camillo Hanks was called "Deaf Charlie."

When Butch was a boy in Beaver, Utah, he had been friends with a rustler named Mike Cassidy. Searching for a man to look up to, young Butch latched on to Mike. Not only did he take Cassidy's name, but he adopted his profession and learned from him the ways to steal horses and rustle cattle.

Butch started out as a horse thief. In 1894, he was caught and sentenced to two years in prison for horse stealing. He was released in 1896 and was fortunate never to see the inside of a prison again.

Even before his imprisonment, Butch had branched out into other areas of crime. On July 24, 1889, he robbed his first bank. With help from Matt Warner and two brothers named Bill and Tom McCarty, he raided the San Miguel Valley Bank in Colorado and made a clean get-away. No one was hurt.

Butch was a thief and guns were the tools of his trade. But, to give him his due, he never killed anyone. He would shoot the horse of anyone chasing him, not the rider.

That could not be said of some of the other members of the gang, however. His sidekick, the Sundance Kid, was certainly a killer. The worst of them all, though, was a cold-blooded outlaw who called himself Kid Curry. He had been a friend of Flatnose George Curry and, like Butch, he had adopted the name of his hero. His real name was Harvey Logan.

The Wild Bunch staged a robbery at a bank in Montpelier, Idaho. Soon afterward, Butch and Elza Lay, (also known as William McGinniss) another member of the gang, brought off another daring robbery. Disguising themselves as miners, they surprised the paymaster at the Castle Gate mine in Utah by thrusting a pistol in his face and demanding the money from the safe. Encouraged by these successes, they robbed a bank in Belle

Fourche, South Dakota. This time they galloped away with $30,000.

With success came unwanted fame. The Wild Bunch was too well known for its own good. Most of the lawmen in the country wanted the glory of capturing them. They even attracted the attention of the famous Pinkerton Detective Agency.

Hoping to take the heat off, The Wild Bunch split up for a time. Butch and Elza Lay went to Alma, New Mexico, where they worked as cowhands for the WS Ranch.

Going straight was hard on Lay. He was captured during a train robbery and sent to prison for life.

In 1899, The Wild Bunch was back in business. They stopped the Union Pacific's Overland Limited and got away with $30,000.

One daring raid followed another. Boldly, they even stopped to have their picture taken after a bank robbery. They sent a copy of it back to the bank with thanks for the contribution to their funds!

It was at this time that Butch decided it would be a good idea to leave the country. That was when he stole the $65,000 in unsigned bills.

Eight years and several bank and train robberies later, Butch and the Sundance Kid found themselves in the country of Bolivia in South America. One rumor has it that they were killed in Bolivia by soldiers. Another claim is that Butch somehow escaped the law in Bolivia and returned safely to the United States.

As for the rest of The Wild Bunch, some were killed and some, like Kid Curry, just plain disappeared. One story goes that Kid Curry was hotly pursued by lawmen after a train robbery in Colorado. Trapped, and not wanting to be taken alive, he committed suicide.

The photograph that the gang sent to a bank they had robbed. With it, went a note of thanks. Left to right standing are Bill Carver and Harry "Kid" Logan. Seated are Harry "Sundance Kid" Longbaugh, Ben Kilpatrick and Butch Cassidy.

GUNS OF THE GUNFIGHTERS

"No law west of the Mississippi, no God west of the Pecos."

So went the old saying. Life was cheap in the Old West. Lawlessness prevailed. Honest citizens knew that they had to be prepared to defend themselves at any time. Most people carried their guns with them as a normal part of their everyday dress. Guns were easy to obtain. A Colt .45 could be bought by mail order for seventeen dollars.

Men who were labelled "gunfighters" could be

The best-selling rifle in the West, the Winchester .44-.40. This 1873 model has an extra rear sight for greater accuracy.

on either side of the law. Some — like Wyatt Earp — tried both sides to see which one was more profitable.

Motion pictures have generally given us an unrealistic view of the Old West. A case in point is the two man gunfight. The classic scene goes like this: two men walk toward each other on a dusty street. The hero waits for the bad guy to draw first and only then does he fire. Such chivalrous behavior would more than likely have resulted in the hero lying dead at the feet of his jubilant killer.

Another false idea is that of the quick-draw dead shot. It was Wild Bill Hickok, a man who never took chances, who said: "Whenever you get into a quarrel be sure and not shoot too quick. I've known many a fellar slip up for shooting in a hurry."

A gunman had to be a real wizard to be both fast and accurate. For one thing, many guns were not accurate when they were fired. Misfires were common, especially with percussion revolvers. Even if a man was fast on the draw, his gun might fail him.

The Remington "Over-and-Under" 0.41, 2-shot model. Over 150,000 were sold.

It was Samuel Colt who was responsible for the most popular revolvers produced during the lawless era of the Old West. He did not invent the revolver; he redesigned the action.

His first two guns were only moderately successful. His first revolver fired six .44 caliber shots instead of the customary five. It was too heavy; it weighed more than four pounds. His next produc-

The Colt .45 of 1873 was, without doubt, the most famous revolver of all time.

tion was the Dragoon or Army revolver which came out in 1848. It was lighter than the first weapon, but still unsatisfactory. It remained in production for only fifteen years.

In 1851, Colt finally got it right. His .36 caliber Navy revolver established Sam Colt's reputation as a master gunmaker. One photograph shows Wild Bill Hickok with two such revolvers in his belt.

In 1873, the Single-Action Army Colt revolver was produced. It was known in western folklore as the "Peacemaker." It became the gunfighters' favorite handgun and is still on sale today.

One of the most colorful Frontier characters active in the pursuit of many notorious outlaws was Charles A. Siringo. He was one of the ace detectives on the Pinkerton payroll.

Charlie Siringo was noted for his gun-play. His favorite guns were the Winchester '73 and the Colt .45. First he used the .44 Henry rimfire caliber Winchester '66 and then the famous .44-40 Model '73. This was the rifle that was called "The Gun That Won the West."

It is often stated that the Colt and the Winchester were the gunfighters' most popular weapons. Of course, there were other gunmakers. Remington and another company, Smith and Wesson, also produced splendid guns. So did the U.S. Government armory at Springfield, Massachusetts.

Last, but by no means least, were the shotguns which were devastating firearms. It is sufficient to say that Doc Holliday's enemies could testify to his marksmanship. He used what he called his "street howitzer," a 10-gauge double shotgun. Remington and Winchester specialized in these destructive guns.

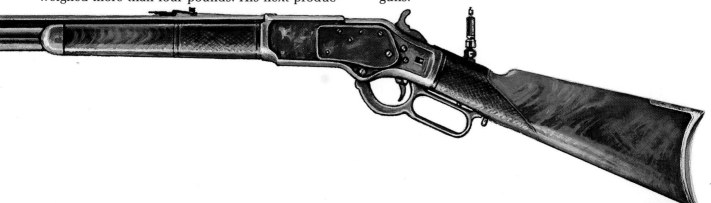

IN THE DAYS OF THE GUNFIGHTERS

1730's   Horses are introduced into the plains, where they flourish. They spread into Canada. Many Indian tribes adopt ponies for transportation and buffalo hunting.

1776   The Declaration of Independence is signed.

1783   The Revolutionary War with Britain comes to an end when the final peace treaty is signed on September 3.

1812   Britain attempts to reclaim the American colonies. The White House is burned. The attempt ends in failure.

1831   Alexis De Tocqueville, a Frenchman, comes to America to explore the new nation. His book, Democracy in America, is a study of the society and politics of the time.

1836   Arkansas becomes a state.

1836   Martin Van Buren is elected president.

1837   Michigan becomes a state and Minnesota is organized as a territory.

1837   The telegraph is invented by Samuel Morse. Morse is also a portrait painter.

1837-1901   The reign of Queen Victoria of Britain.

1855   The Free Soil convention drafts an anti-slavery constitution.

1858   The first stage coach line to the west coast begins. It originates in St. Louis.

1860   The Pony Express begins a mail run from Missouri to California.

1861   Abraham Lincoln is elected president.

1861   Confederates fire on Fort Sumter, beginning the Civil War. In the south it is called the War Between The States.

1861   The telegraph links the country from east coast to west coast.

1862   The Homestead Act encourages settlement in the west, closing the wide open spaces.

1865   General Lee, leader of the Confederate army, surrenders to General Ulysses S. Grant, leader of the Union army. They meet at Appomattox on April 9. The Civil War ends.

1865   President Lincoln is assassinated at Ford's Theatre on April 14.

1874   The James/Younger gang begins robbing trains.

1881   The governor of New Mexico, Lew Wallace, signs Billy the Kid's death warrant.

1900   The census finds the population of the U.S. is a little over 75,000,000.

1900   The Wright Brothers build their first glider.

1901   Oil is discovered in Texas, causing a boom in that state.

1902   Buffalo Bill takes his Wild West show to Great Britain, where it is a huge success.